2015

I0412098

PLAN OF BATTLE: UKRAINE

PERRY JONES

Plan of Battle: Ukraine presents a Plan of Battle for the Ukraine government that can win the battle for eastern Ukraine. Written by Perry Jones, the author of the November 1990 Plan of Battle: Iraq that was 95% identical to the February 1991 Gulf War and Plan of Battle: Bosnia that was 100% identical to the plan that won the war for the allies during the Serbian-Bosnian Conflict in the mid and late 90s.

Perry Jones
Kearsedge Boston
4/1/2015

PLAN OF BATTLE: UKRAINE

Plan of Battle: Ukraine

Copyright 2015 by Perry Jones - All Rights Reserved

ISBN-13: 978-1511548380

ISBN-10: 151154838X

Perry Jones is the author of the Plan of Battle: Iraq that was 95% identical to the operations that followed in February of 1991. Mr. Jones' Plan of Battle estimated combat operations of 100 to 1,000 hours in length depending upon the degree of Iraq resistance and Allied casualties of 750 with approximately 50% occurring as a result of a planned amphibious assault upon the Umm Qasr. "Official" estimates were predicting 10,000 to 30,000 Allied casualties and a war from 3 to 6 months in duration.

Author also of Plan of Battle: Bosnia that was delivered to then President Clinton, the Vice President, the NATO Commander and the Joint Chiefs, Mr. Jones' Plan was 100% identical to the campaign that followed and which brought the war to an end in just a few days with just one Allied casualty, (Mr. Jones forecast 14).

You may contact Mr. Jones at
PerryJones@KearsedgeBoston.com

OTHER BOOKS BY PERRY JONES

Investing in the Future:
A Policy for the Next President

The Book of Revelation:
An Interpretation for Today

The Book of Revelation Workbook

Poems and Dreams: A Sampler

Hyperspace Calculations

God's Plan for You

God's Laws – The Itemization

Proof of the Existence of God

Why Does God Allow Suffering?

$300,000 a Day

7 Secrets of High Yield Returns with Low Risk

Real Estate Investing: Tips, Myths and Realities

PLAN OF BATTLE: UKRAINE

Plan of Battle: Ukraine

Introduction

Can a war with Russia be won? No. Can a war for the eastern provinces be won? Without question, yes, as this plan will demonstrate.

I develop Plans of Battle that work and attain the results required.

Plan of Battle: Iraq

I developed a Plan of Battle: Iraq for the 1991 Gulf War which was 95% identical to the war which followed. I forecast 750 combat casualties for the Coalition forces while others were predicting estimates as high as 30,000. Most people expected combat casualties to number around 10,000. Actual Coalition casualties numbered approximately 250.

I estimated that the war would last from 100 to 1,000 hours based on the degree of Iraqi resistance. Others estimated the war would last anywhere from 3 to 6 months. The ground war lasted exactly 100 hours.

I planned a Marine assault northward into Kuwait from staging areas in Saudi Arabia to act as a "fixing force" to hold Iraqi combat elements in place while a left hook armored assault would occur in the desert some 200 kilometers or so to the west. This is exactly what happened.

I also planned a Marine amphibious assault to land 30 kilometers upriver from the Gulf near Basra. I expected from one half to two thirds of all casualties to result from this assault alone. This assault was not implemented by the U.S. or Coalition forces and the number of combat casualties reflect this.

Plan of Battle: Bosnia

Based on the success of the air campaign in the Gulf War of 1991, I planned an all-air campaign against Serbian forces during the Bosnian-Serbian conflict of the mid and late 1990's. I sent this Plan of Battle to then U.S. President Clinton, the U.S. Vice President, and Chairman of the Joint Chiefs of Staff.

The 1999 action which followed and stopped the war dead in its tracks was 100% identical to the Plan of Battle I had developed. The only difference between my plan and the results I calculated was that I forecast combat casualties for U.S. and NATO forces at 14 while actual casualties numbered only one.

I develop Plans of Battle that work and attain the results required.

The following is my Plan of Battle for Ukraine.

Objective

The objective of this plan of battle is to defeat enemy forces in eastern Ukraine forcing their withdrawal from Ukraine through the implementation of maneuver warfare.

Maneuver warfare is herein defined as the motion of combat elements through the dimensions of space, time and thought at an operational tempo greater than that of the opposing force. In Ukraine, the political and public dimensions must also be considered through the means of public relations, traditional media and social media, but these will not be considered in this Plan of Battle.

Enemy forces are defined as units operating in opposition to the objectives of the national government of Ukraine. This may include rebel and separatist factions as well as regular Russian forces.

Repositioning

Because of the fluidity and dynamics of the current situation and the paucity of information flowing from Ukraine, I have no idea where Ukrainian combat forces are currently situated. But if I had a choice, I would move:

72nd Mechanized Brigade east to support combat operations in the eastern theater

30th Mechanized Brigade east to support combat operations

51st Mechanized Brigade east to occupy the position vacated by the 72nd

24th Mechanized Brigade northeast to occupy the position vacated by the 30th

128th Guards north to occupy the position vacated by the 24th and to protect the western flank

This may or may not have already occurred and current troop dispositions may be entirely different from what I assume above.

Political Repositioning

Regardless of the presence of Russian troops and arms joining the rebels in eastern Ukraine, the strategic objectives of this plan would not be improved or realized by Ukrainian assertions that Russians forces are involved in the fighting. Let this matter simmer out and avoid discussion. The reason for this is that this Plan will smash Russian troops in the area and drive them out. If we leave a channel open for Putin to quietly remove his forces he may do so, but if Ukraine continues to claim that Russian troops are present, Putin may consider it his duty and obligation to win the battle (even though he claims no Russian forces are present) – Ukraine does not want this.

Reconstitution

Ukrainian forces should be rebuilt around a highly mobile armored force of heavy attack capacity and lethal force. In The United States, this capability is held by Cavalry regiments.

Building on this concept, and using these units as the core, Ukraine should build out the following units:

92nd Mechanized Brigade

93rd Mechanized Brigade

17th Armored

72nd Mechanized Brigade

30th Mechanized Brigade

These units will be structured around the concept of a heavy cavalry. Utilizing the cavalry designation:

5 Cavalry Regiments of 3 armored squadrons and 1 air squadron each.

At the Regimental level there will be the following units:

1 Headquarters & Personnel Services

1 Support Squadron

1 Combat Engineer Company

1 Military Intelligence Company

1 Chemical (NBC) Company

1 Air Defense Company

1 Artillery Brigade

1 Aviation Command

1 Mechanized Infantry Command

1 Anti-Tank Command

Each armored squadron would consist of 12 companies each plus attached units:

3 cavalry troops

1 tank company

1 artillery battery

1 helicopter company

1 air defense company

1 anti-tank mechanized infantry company

1 headquarters company

1 medical unit

1 maintenance company

1 support and transportation company

1 military intelligence company

1 military police company

1 chemical (NBC) warfare company

1 combat engineers company

1 special forces company

1 mechanized infantry company

1 drone section

Each cavalry Regiment will consist of two types of units – Integrated Units and Independently Operating Units.

Integrated Units

Integrated units are spread across the combat forces as required and necessary to complete the mission. These integrated units include:

1 Air Defense company

1 Chemical Warfare company

Independently Operating Units

Independently operating units would operate as a unit commanded by the Squadron Commander.

    3 Cavalry Troops

    1 Tank Company

    1 Artillery Battery

    1 Helicopter Troop

    1 Anti-Tank Mechanized Infantry

    1 Headquarters and Personnel Services Company

    1 Medical Unit

    1 Maintenance Company

    1 Support and Transportation Company

    1 Military Intelligence Company

    1 Military Police Company

    1 Combat Engineers Company

    1 Chemical (NBC) Warfare Company

    1 Special Forces Company

    1 Mechanized Infantry Company

1 Drone Company

The objective of this reconstitution is to create a combined arms corps capable of meeting and defeating rebel and Russian forces in the field. This will take time, money and training to accomplish, but it can be done. While that is underway, the regiments should have no less than one all tank company with three armored combat vehicle companies with as many tanks in each of these as can be added.

Utilizing American tables of organization for maximum mobility and lethality we establish:

   1 Tank Company = 14 tanks

   1 Cavalry Troop = 10 units

   1 Headquarters Platoon
        1 tank
        1 ACV
        1 command track

   2 Scout Platoons
        6 ACV each

2 Tank Platoons
>   4 tanks each

1 Mortar Section
>   2 tracked mortar carriers

1 Maintenance Platoon
>   1 truck
>   1 tracked maintenance
>   1 car/jeep

1 Medical Section
>   1 tracked medical ambulance
>   1 car/jeep/Humvee

1 Chemical Warfare
>   1 tracked chemical warfare
>   1 truck
>   1 car/jeep/Humvee

1 Air Defense
>   2 air defense artillery tracks
>   2 ammunition carriers, tracked

1 Artillery Battery
>   8 self-propelled artillery
>   8 ammunition carriers, tracked
>   2 car/jeep/Humvee
>   3 command tracks

1 command track
> 1 fire direction track
> 1 communications track (reserve)

1 Helicopter Troop
> 4 attack helicopters
> 4 scout helicopters
> 1 observation helicopter
> 1 transport helicopter

1 Air Defense Artillery
> 1 command track
> 4 air defense artillery tracks, heavy
> 4 air defense artillery tracks, other
> 2 tracked ammunition carriers
> 2 car/jeep/Humvee
> 2 trucks

1 Anti-Tank Mechanized Infantry
> 8 anti-tank ACV
> 8 personnel carrier ACV
> 4 trucks
> 4 ammunition carriers, tracked
> 2 car/jeep/Humvee

1 Medical Unit
> 2 car/jeep/Humvee
> 2 trucks
> 4 medical ambulances, tracked

2 supply tracks

2 other vehicles

1 Maintenance Company

2 tank recovery vehicles, tracked

3 maintenance tracks

4 heavy wreckers

2 tractor trailers

4 heavy trucks

2 car/jeep/Humvee

1 command vehicle

1 Support and Transportation Company

4 ordnance tracks

16 Humvees

24 medium trucks (2.5 ton)

22 water tankers

30 5 ton trucks

1 Military Intelligence Company

6 Humvee mobile electronics suites

4 tracked electronic stations

Other equipment and tracks as
required

1 Military Police Company

3 1 ¼ ton trucks

1 wrecker

3 cargo trucks

29 light armored trucks
15 armored security Humvees
2 Humvees

1 Combat Engineers Company
12 APCs
6 armored earthmoving tracks
3 armored vehicle-launched bridges
3 combat engineer vehicles
6 heavy dump trucks
1 scoop loader
4 Humvee mobile canteens
Assorted other excavating,
entrenching & combat engineer
vehicles & tracks

1 NBC Warfare Company
6 NBC Reconnaissance vehicles
7 tracked smoke generators
2 mobile decontamination stations
4 Humvees
Other assorted detection and
decontamination vehicles

1 Special Forces Company
Equipment as designated by
Regimental Command

1 Mechanized Infantry Company
   4 Humvees
   12 APCs
   4 Anti-tank missile tracks

1 Drone Company
   4 scout drones
   2 long range scout drones
   2 stealth scout drones
   4 rocket attack drones
   4 missile drones
   1 command track
   2 fire control tracks
   2 air defense artillery tracks
   2 maintenance tracks
   4 trucks
   4 other vehicles

1 Helicopter Squadron – Air Cavalry
  1 Headquarters Troop
    3 heavy transport helicopters
    3 electronic warfare helicopters
    1 scout helicopters

  3 Scout Troops
    6 scout helicopters
    4 attack helicopters

2 Helicopter Attack Troops
>4 scout helicopters
>8 attack helicopters

1 Transport Troop
>15 heavy transport helicopters

1 Maintenance Troop
>2 transport helicopters
>4 trucks
>2 maintenance tracks
>4 other vehicle

1 Medical Section
>4 air ambulance helicopters

Combat support forces would provide logistics for all fielded units.

Training

Ideally, training should occur over a period of two to three years in a stable, non-threat environment. Because of the current situation, this is impossible and, although initial training should be, whenever possible, in areas situated outside of combat areas, advanced training will be in the form of actual combat. Unfortunately, this will cause losses to men and equipment which would otherwise be avoided if there was no immediate threat.

Training will consist of 4 phases:

Immediately after the reconstitution of forces as described above, Phase 1 of training will commence:

Phase 1 – Individual Unit Training – 30 days

Units will train outside of combat areas if possible allowing unit commanders and enlisted personnel to learn to work and communicate together as a group.

Day 1

12 hours lecture training
Lecture training will focus on the current

situation, why rebel and Russian forces must be – and will be defeated – the procedures, protocol and communications protocol of each unit, combat first aid training, equipment and weapons training, and other lecture training as may be determined by the unit/squadron commanders.

12 hours rest

Day 2

4 hours lecture training
8 hours field and equipment training
12 hours rest

Day 3

2 hours lecture training
10 hours field training
2 hours debriefing (after action reports and evaluation)
10 hours rest

Day 4

24 hours rest

Days 5 - 8

10 hours field training
2 hours debriefing
12 hours rest

Day 9

      12 hours lecture/debriefing

      12 hours rest

Days 10 – 12

      14 hours field training

      2 hours debriefing

      8 hours rest

Day 13

      4 hours field training

      2 hours lecture/debriefing

      18 hours rest

Days 14 – 18

      14 hours field training

      3 hours debriefing

      7 hours rest

Day 19

      5 hours field training

      2 hours debriefing

      17 hours rest

Days 20 – 25

      16 hours field training

      8 hours rest

Day 26
>8 hours lecture/debriefing
>16 hours rest

Days 27 – 29
>20 hours field training
>4 hours rest

Day 30
>24 hours rest

Phase 2 – Squadron Level Training – 30 Days

Day 1 – Squadrons meet as squadrons for first time
>5 hours lecture/debriefing – lessons learned from Phase 1
>19 hours enlisted rest
>5 hours officer lecture/debriefing
>14 hours officer's rest

Days 2 – 5
>2 hours lecture – what will happen in squadron level training
>8 hours field training
>2 hours debriefing
>12 hours rest

Days 6 – 7
>12 hours field training
>2 hours debriefing
>10 hours rest

Day 8
>5 hours field training
>2 hours debriefing
>17 hours rest

Days 9 – 15
>15 hours field training
>2 hours debriefing
>7 hours rest

Day 16
>9 hours rest
>4 hours lecture/debriefing
>2 hours field training
>9 hours rest

Days 17 – 20
>17 hours field training
>1 hour debriefing
>6 hours rest

Day 21
>8 hours field training

4 hours debriefing
12 hours rest

Days 22 – 25
    18 hours field training
    6 hours rest

Day 26
    24 hours rest

Day 27
    4 hours debriefing
    8 hours field training
    12 hours rest

Days 28 – 29
    20 hours field training
    4 hours rest

Day 30
    22 hours rest
    2 hours debriefing

Phase 3 – Regimental Training Level – Combat Operations – Forces will employ hit and run tactics against lightly guarded enemy positions and weak enemy forces.

Artillery will employ "shoot-and-scoot" tactics.

Helicopter units will employ "Run-in, Pop-up, Attack, Exit" tactics.

Special forces and forward observers are pre-positioned and will select targets.

Drone units may select targets and employ "hit-and-run" tactics.

Days 1 – 3
> Movement to position as needed
> 4 hours officer debriefing +-
> 2 hours enlisted debriefing +- as needed
> Establish targets
> Reemphasize defense plans
> Articulate exit strategy
> Establish rendezvous points

Day 4
> Attack initial position
> Execute exit strategy
> Rendezvous at rendezvous points

Day 5

Transition to rearward assembly
points
Assess and evaluate operations
Select next targets

Day 6

4 hours field training against specific
targets
Resupply, replenish and repair
2 hours debriefing

Day 7

Movement to position

Days 8 - 9

Attack selected targets
Execute exit strategy as needed
De-occupy one position*
Meet at rendezvous points

Day 10

Assess and evaluate
Select next targets
Replenish, resupply and repair

Day 11 – 12

Movement to position

Days 13 – 14

    Attack selected targets
    Execute exit strategy when necessary
    Meet at rendezvous points

Day 15

    Transition to rearward area
    Assess and evaluate
    Debriefings
    Replenish, resupply and repair
    Select next targets

Days 16 - 17

    Movement to position

Days 18 – 20

    Attack selected targets
    Execute exit strategy
    Meet at rendezvous points
    Regroup
    Attack next target package
    Execute exit strategy
    Meet at rendezvous points
    Regroup
    Attack third target package
    Execute exit strategy
    De-occupy second position*
    Meet at rendezvous points
    Transition to rearward areas

Days 21 – 28
>Rest
>Replenish, resupply & repair
>Assess and evaluate
>Select next targets
>Prepare battle campaign
>Equip forces as needed

Day 29
>Briefing

Day 30
>24 hours rest

*De-occupy Positions – De-occupying positions is necessary to imbue the enemy with over-confidence and convince them in coming operations, that Ukraine forces are defeatable causing them to over-estimate their own capabilities and underestimate Ukrainian forces. As a result, they will position their forces and use tactics in such a manner that will force high casualty rates on their side while minimizing losses to our own.

Pre-Positioning

Special forces will function as scouts and target selection only.

Special forces will train from Days 1 through 10 of Phase 1 and move to position from Days 11 to 15.

Throughout Days 16 – 30 of Phase 1 and throughout all of Phase 2, special forces will select targets and move independently across the countryside unobserved by enemy forces.

Objective of these forces is to initially select weak and vulnerable forces, positions, command centers, logistics nodes and vulnerable geographical points and supply lines that can be easily defeated and neutralized with easy, safe exits by friendly forces.

During Phase 2, forward observers and intelligence operatives will be recruited from among the local population in the planned areas of operations to select targets, forward enemy troop movements and dispositions and identify commands and units.

Men and women from age 40 and older are the best candidates for these groups because they are the least likely to be suspected by the enemy, especially women.

During Phase 3 and onward, these resources will be activated to support combat operations.

Pre-positioning

>5 Armored Cavalry Regiments

>Regular Army Infantry

>Regular Army Artillery

>Tactical Air Support

Pre-positioning will consist of 3 pre-positioning movements representing 3 separate campaigns. This will flow into a fourth primary combat effort with a coordinated attack by elements of all Ukrainian forces in theater.

Campaign 1

Force 1
Pre-position 3 cavalry regiments 10 to 20 kilometers northwest enemy forward positions.

Force 2
Pre-position 2 cavalry regiments 10 to 20
kilometers west of enemy forward positions 50 to
75 kilometers southwest of Force 1.

Campaign 2

Pre-positioning of forces for Campaign 2 is
dependent upon the results of the first campaign but
will also be divided into 2 forces.

Force 1
Pre-position 3 cavalry regiments 10 to 20
kilometers west of enemy forward positions at
approximately center of former enemy territory
held.

Force 2
Pre-position 2 cavalry regiments 10 to 20
kilometers west of enemy forward positions
approximately 50 kilometers south or southwest of
Force 1.

Campaign 3

Force 1

Pre-position 3 cavalry regiments 10 to 20 kilometers west of enemy forward positions within 15 to 20 kilometers of Mariupol.

Force 2

Acts as a reserve, will be held at a position 10 to 25 kilometers southwest of Force 1.

Operations

Objective of operations is to inflict damage to enemy forces by attacking critical enemy infrastructure whether this is troops, equipment, logistical, communications, command and control or psychological forcing the enemy to withdraw from the field and cease combat operations.

Each of the first three campaigns are to be rapid, violent assaults which begin and end quickly and in which friendly forces leave the field of combat to rendezvous at rally points distant and safe from enemy counter and air attack.

Campaign 1, Force 1

Force 1 attacks southeast into enemy forces turning westward to meet Force 2. Artillery provides shoot and scoot tactics engaging targets as requested by Force 1 commander. Air cavalry supports or leads ground assault as determined by Force 1 commander or as events warrant as determined by individual air commanders.

Campaign 1, Force 2

Force 2 attacks eastward, initiating hostilities 2 hours after Force 1 engages enemy forces. Artillery provides shoot and scoot tactics engaging targets as requested by Force 2 commander. Air cavalry supports or leads ground assault as determined by Force 2 commander or as events warrant as determined by individual air commanders.

Campaign 1 – Denouement

Force 1 & 2 link up and retire westward off the field of battle and 20 to 30 kilometers away from the nearest enemy forces. Air defense artillery provides air security while regular Army infantry provides location security.

Campaign 2, Force 1

Force 1 attacks east for a distance of 10 to 20 kilometers turning south for a further distance of 20 to 30 kilometers or until link up with Force 2. Artillery provides shoot and scoot tactics engaging targets as requested by Force 1 commander. Air cavalry supports or leads ground assault as determined by Force 1 commander or as events warrant as determined by individual air commanders.

Campaign 2, Force 2

Force 2 attacks east for a distance of 20 to 25 kilometers turning north for a distance of 10 to 20 kilometers or until link up with Force 1. Artillery provides shoot and scoot tactics engaging targets as requested by Force 2 commander. Air cavalry supports or leads ground assault as determined by Force 2 commander or as events warrant as determined by individual air commanders.

Campaign 2 – Denouement

Upon link up, Forces 1 & 2 fight west for a distance of 30 to 40 kilometers or until safely away from enemy forces. Continue to rendezvous point as determined by Regimental Commander. Air defense artillery provides air security while regular Army infantry provides location security.

Campaign 3, Force 1

In the vicinity of Mariupol, Force 1 attacks the flank of enemy forces forcing enemy into a turning movement. Air cavalry attacks visible enemy ground forces while artillery attacks targets as requested by Force 1 and Air Cavalry commanders.

Campaign 3, Force 2

In position as a reserve component only, Force 2 enters combat to support Force 1 or to attack select targets only upon command of Regimental Commander.

Campaign 3 – Denouement

Force 1 disengages and maneuvers west avoiding enemy contact if possible to rendezvous point selected by Regimental Command. Air defense artillery provides air security while regular Army infantry provides location security.

Primary Operation, Campaign 4

Pre-Positioning

1 Cavalry Regiment will be used as a reserve along with elements of regular Army and artillery.

Elements of tactical air, regular Army, Mechanized Brigades and Artillery will pre-position in 3 formations approximately equidistant from each other along the front of enemy forces at a distance of 15 to 20 kilometers from the enemy. Forces may be separated from 20 to 50 kilometers apart.

Each formation will be spearheaded by a Cavalry Regiment with 2 cavalry regiments forming the spearhead of the formation expecting to meet the greatest number of enemy forces.

Special forces and intelligence units will reposition to capture enemy data, force structure, troop movements, logistics details and control, communications and command points and relay this information to the Regimental command.

Operations

By hour as minimum time, by day as maximum time required.

Hour 1 (Day 1)

> Tactical air will engage enemy targets.
> Artillery moves up to attack positions.

Hour 2 (Day 1)

> Tactical air stands down to replenish and assess damage.

Artillery engages enemy targets.
Each formation moves up to within 5 to 9
kilometers from the enemy's expected
forward positions.

Hour 3 (Day 1)

Artillery stands down.
Formations move forward and attack
eastward.
Tactical air supports ground operations.
Artillery supports ground operations as
directed.

Hours 4 – 10 (Day 1, 2)

Formations continue forward (east)
engaging and neutralizing enemy forces and
seizing tactical objectives.

Hour 11 (Day 1, 2)

Wheel-Back

Formations attempt to outflank enemy
positions.

Tactical air and artillery support ground
offensive.

Hours 12 – 15 (Day 1, 2, 3)

> Formations press forward (east) to pre-determined objectives.

> Tactical air and artillery support ground offensive.

Hours 15 – 17 (Day 1, 2, 3)

> Formations seize and secure objectives and prepare to defend objectives from enemy attack.

> Tactical air and artillery support ground offensive.

Hours 17 – 21 (Day 1, 2, 3, 4)

> Formations build-up defenses around objectives.

> Tactical air and artillery support ground offensive.

Hour 22 (Day 2, 3, 4, 5)

Stand-down, cease-fire.

> If enemy agrees, a cease-fire is implemented and new forward positions are consolidated as friendly territory.

Final

Ukraine government meets with rebel and Russian counterparts to discuss and agree upon cessation of hostilities and establish territorial lines.

While no Plan of Battle is perfect and every plan survives only until first contact with the enemy, this Plan of Battle has been written to assure the greatest chance of victory for Ukraine forces in the eastern Ukraine theater of operations against enemy (Russian and rebel) forces.

References

Clancy, Tom – *Armored Cav - A Guided Tour of an Armored Cavalry Regiment* Berkley Books, Berkley Publishing Company, 1994

FM 100-5 U.S. Army Operations Manual, Headquarters, Department of the Army, 1993

FM 17-95 Cavalry Operations, Headquarters, Department of the Army, 1996

ADP 3-05 Special Operations Manual, Headquarters, Department of the Army, 2012

MCDP 1-0 Marine Corps Operations, Department of the Navy, Headquarters, United States Marine Corps, 2001

Warfighting, United States Marine Corps, Bantam Doubleday Dell Publishing Company, 1984

44

www.ingramcontent.com/pod-product-compliance
Lightning Source LLC
Chambersburg PA
CBHW070500290526
45790CB00003B/1027